Level E • Book 3

QuickReads®

A Research-Based Fluency Program

Elfrieda H. Hiebert, Ph.D.

D1303092

MODERN CURRICULUM PRESS
Pearson Learning Group

Program Reviewers and Consultants

Dr. Barbara A. Baird
Director of Federal Programs/Richardson ISD
Richardson, TX

Dr. Kate Kinsella
Dept. of Secondary Education and Step to College Program
San Francisco State University
San Francisco, CA

Pat Sears
Early Child Coordinator/Virginia Beach Public Schools
Virginia Beach, VA

Dr. Judith B. Smith
Supervisor of ESOL and World and Classical Languages/Baltimore City Public Schools
Baltimore, MD

The following people have contributed to the development of this product:

Art and Design: David Mager, Salita Mehta, Evelyn O'Shea, Dan Thomas, Dan Trush, Karolyn Wehner

Editorial: Lynn W. Kloss

Manufacturing: Michele Uhl

Marketing: Alison Bruno

Production: Jeffrey Engel, Roxanne Knoll, Phyllis Rosinsky

Publishing Operations: Jennifer Van Der Heide

1-800-321-3106
www.pearsonlearning.com

Contents

Contents

SCIENCE **The Laws of Motion**

Contents

The American Civil War

Contents

Acknowledgments

All photography © Pearson Education, Inc. (PEI) unless otherwise specifically noted.

Cover: © Wally McNamee/Corbis. 3: © Mark Burnett/Stock, Boston, Inc./PictureQuest. 4: Taxi/Getty Images, Inc. 5: Jim Collins/Getty Images, Inc. 6: Peter Adams/FPG International LLC/Getty Images. 7: The Granger Collection, New York. 8: Bruce Stoddard/Getty Images, Inc. 10: Bob Daemmrich/Bob Daemmrich Photography. 12: © Maxine Hall/Corbis. 14: © Mark Burnett/Stock, Boston, Inc./PictureQuest. 16: Jeff Smith/The Image Bank/Getty Images, Inc.; 24: Marc Romanelli/ The Image Bank/Getty Images, Inc. 26: © Lowell Georgia/Corbis. 28: SuperStock/ PictureQuest. 30: Doug Menuez/Getty Images, Inc. 32: Taxi/Getty Images, Inc. 38: © J-L Charmet/Photo Researchers, Inc. 40: © George H.H. Huey/Corbis. 42: Jim Collins/Getty Images, Inc. 44: © Roger Ressmeyer/Corbis. 46: © David Stoecklein/Corbis. 52: Peter Adams/FPG International LLC/Getty Images. 54: © Giraudon/Art Resource, NY. 56: © Gustavo Tomsich/Corbis. 58: The Granger Collection, New York. 60: © Bettmann/Corbis. 66: *t.* © 2000 North Wind Picture Archives; *b.* © Gianni Dagli Orti/Corbis. 68: The Granger Collection, New York. 70: *t.* Schomburg Center for Research in Black Culture; *b.* © Bettman/Corbis. 72: Hulton Archive/Getty Images Inc. 74: © Bettmann/Corbis. 80: © Jonathan Blair/Corbis. 82: Nick Nicholson/Getty Images, Inc. 84: Bruce Stoddard/Getty Images, Inc. 86: © Jeremy Horner/Corbis. 88: *t.* Jack Parsons/Omni-Photo Communications, Inc.; *b.* Hopi Learning Centre/DK Images.

How Light Works

The light from candle flames travels in visible wavelengths.

The Colors of Light

Candle flames, light bulbs, and the Sun are three light sources. Light from these sources acts partly like a wave. Waves [25] of many different lengths are contained in sunlight.

The human eye can sense different colors for light waves of different lengths. The longest wavelength that [50] people can see appears as the color red. As the wavelengths of light get shorter, people see orange, yellow, green, blue, indigo, and violet. People [75] cannot see wavelengths longer than those in red light or shorter than those in violet light. When you see a rainbow in the sky, what [100] you see is all of the wavelengths of light separated into bands of color.

Light that contains all of the visible wavelengths appears to be [125] white. If the eye receives no light in the visible range, people see only black. [140]

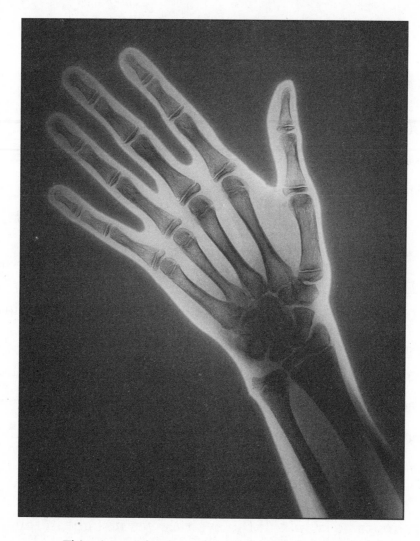

This picture shows an X-ray of a person's hand.
X-rays are one kind of invisible light wave.

The Speed of Light

At about 186,000 miles per second, light travels faster than anything else on Earth. At this speed, light can circle Earth [25] almost eight times in one second. Light only travels through space at this speed. It travels more slowly through matter, such as water and glass. [50]

Light waves travel in straight lines in all directions. Although light waves can travel through some solid objects, such waves are reflected, or bounced back, [75] from most objects.

Visible light waves make up a small portion of all the light waves that exist. Some light waves are invisible and can [100] travel through solid objects. For example, the waves that carry radio signals have longer wavelengths than visible light and can pass through walls. X-rays, too, [125] are invisible. They are much shorter than visible light waves and can pass through the human body. [142]

Because the cat's body is opaque, it makes a shadow on the floor.

Light and Shadows

When light shines on an object, one of three things happens: The light passes through the object easily, it passes through the[25] object but is scattered, or it is blocked. Because air and glass are transparent, light waves move through them without scattering. Images can be seen[50] clearly through transparent objects. That is why windows and eyeglasses are made of glass.

A second group of objects lets light waves through, but scatters[75] the waves. Such objects, including plastic bottles, are translucent. You can see images, but not clear details, through translucent objects.

Objects that block light completely[100] are called opaque. Opaque objects do not let any light through them. When you place an opaque object near a light source, you see a[125] shadow that is shaped like the object. Because your hand is opaque, it makes a shadow near a lamp.[144]

Lasers are used in stores to read the bar codes on products.

Laser Beams

Usually, light contains waves of many different wavelengths that travel in all directions. By creating a beam of light waves that are exactly[25] the same wavelength, a powerful form of light called a laser is produced.

There are several ways to create laser beams. One way to create[50] a laser beam is with a tube that has mirrors at both ends and is filled with a special gas. An electric current causes the[75] gas to give off light waves. These light waves all have the same wavelength. The mirrors in the tube help produce more light waves that[100] are traveling in the same direction. This light beam exits the tube as a laser.

Lasers are used to read bar codes on products in[125] stores and to play music in CD players. Some laser beams are even strong enough to cut through steel.[144]

How Light Works

Even though this straw is straight, it seems to bend at the surface of the water in the glass.

Light Tricks

Light waves travel in straight lines. However, when light waves move from air to a material like glass or water, the direction of[25] the light can change. The path of light can refract, or bend.

The refraction of light can play tricks on your eyes. For example, look[50] at a straw in a glass of water. A straight straw seems to bend at the surface of the water because the light waves change[75] direction when they enter the water.

Refraction can cause travelers in a desert to see mirages of water and trees. The water and trees may[100] exist. However, if they do exist, they may be far away. In the desert, the hottest and lightest air is closest to the ground. As[125] light waves move closer to the ground, they refract, or bend. This refracted light can create a mirage.[143]

How Light Works

Write words that will help you remember what you learned.

The Colors of Light

_____

_____

_____

_____

The Speed of Light

_____

_____

_____

_____

Light and Shadows

_____

_____

_____

_____

Laser Beams

_____

_____

_____

_____

Light Tricks

_____

_____

_____

_____

The Colors of Light

1. How do human eyes sense colors?

   Ⓐ as waves of light that are in rainbow shapes

   Ⓑ as bands of light that come from candles

   Ⓒ as waves of light that are at certain lengths

   Ⓓ as rays that are in the Sun's light

2. What do you see when you see a rainbow?

   _____

   _____

   _____

The Speed of Light

1. How do light waves travel?

   Ⓐ in light waves that circle the Earth

   Ⓑ in invisible radio signals with long wavelengths

   Ⓒ in straight lines in all directions

   Ⓓ in X-rays that pass through the human body

2. What are two kinds of invisible light waves?

   _____

   _____

   _____

How Light Works

Light and Shadows

1. How is a shadow formed?

   Ⓐ by scattering light through a plastic bottle

   Ⓑ by blocking light with an opaque object

   Ⓒ by using glass to scatter light waves

   Ⓓ by blocking light with a transparent object

2. What three things can happen when light shines on an object? Why do they happen?

   _____

   _____

   _____

Laser Beams

1. A laser beam is made up of _____

   Ⓐ light waves that are all traveling at the same wavelength.

   Ⓑ electric currents that are bouncing around inside a tube.

   Ⓒ bar codes that are on products in stores.

   Ⓓ CD players that play sound recordings with mirrors.

2. Describe two things lasers can do.

   _____

   _____

   _____

Light Tricks

1. Light is refracted because light waves _____

   Ⓐ move more quickly through water than through air.

   Ⓑ are made of different kinds of light.

   Ⓒ bend when they change direction.

   Ⓓ travel in straight lines through all materials.

2. Why does a straight straw seem to bend in water?

   _____

   _____

   _____

Connect Your Ideas

1. Describe two ways people use light every day.

   _____

   _____

   _____

2. Suppose there was another passage on this topic. Would you expect it to be about different kinds of light bulbs or about how sound waves work? Why?

   _____

   _____

   _____

Heat and Energy

Running up stairs generates heat in your body.

Generating Heat

When your hands feel cold, you rub them together to make them feel warm. Rubbing your hands together moves the particles in your[25] hands. The faster you rub your hands, the faster the particles move. The faster the particles move, the warmer your hands become. As the particles[50] move against one another, they create a force called friction. The friction between your hands creates heat.

Wherever there is heat, energy is being generated.[75] When you rub your hands together, you generate energy. You generate energy in other ways, too. When you run, ride your bicycle, or climb stairs,[100] your body changes the food you eat into energy. The heat that you feel in your body after running, riding your bicycle, or going up[125] stairs comes from the energy that your body has generated. Your body generates and uses energy all the time.[144]

Heat and Energy

A thermometer shows when the temperature is safe for these chicks.

Temperature

Temperature is a measure of how hot or cold something is. When you eat ice cream outside on a hot day, it melts. This [25] is because the ice cream is cold and the air is hot.

The tools that measure temperature are called thermometers. Thermometers can be used to [50] measure the temperature of our bodies, of the air, and of food. Some thermometers have a thin tube with liquid inside. When the temperature gets [75] warmer, the liquid moves up in the tube. When the temperature gets colder, the liquid moves down in the tube. Marks on the tube show [100] the temperature in degrees on a scale. The degree at which the liquid stops shows the temperature.

Many people place thermometers outside their homes to [125] measure the temperature of the air. As the temperature goes up, so does the liquid in the thermometer. [143]

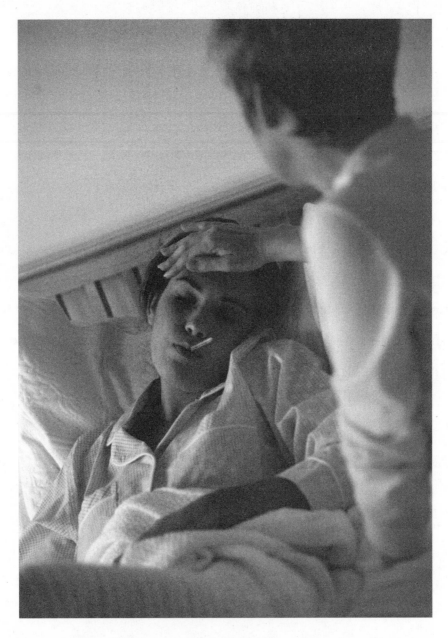

In addition to showing the temperature of the air,
thermometers also show if a person has a fever.

Growing Larger and Smaller

Why does the liquid in a thermometer go up when you have a fever? Liquids expand, or get bigger, when they [25] are heated. The liquid in the thermometer expands because the temperature in your mouth is higher than usual. If you put the thermometer into cold [50] water, the liquid contracts, or gets smaller.

Liquids expand and contract because they are made of moving molecules. When molecules get hot, they move farther [75] apart. When molecules cool, they move closer together. In this way, liquids seem to grow and shrink when the temperature changes.

Many things expand and [100] contract. Sidewalks expand when it's hot and contract when it's cool. When concrete and other materials expand, they often expand unevenly. Some parts expand more [125] quickly than others. Building sidewalks in small concrete pieces keeps them from cracking when they expand unevenly. [142]

Heat and Energy

Wearing light-colored clothes in summer helps you stay cool.
Wearing dark-colored clothes in winter helps you stay warm.

Heat in Black and White

People who live in hot climates often wear white or light-colored clothes. People who live in cold climates often [25] wear black or dark-colored clothes. This is because white clothes make you feel cool, but black clothes make you feel hot.

White and black [50] materials work with light in different ways. Light bounces off white clothes, so it is cooler to wear white clothes in hot weather. In contrast, [75] light is absorbed, or soaked up, by black clothes. When the particles in the material absorb light, they move around. As the particles move against [100] one another, they create friction, and the material heats up. That's why you feel hot when you wear a black shirt on a hot day. [125] It makes sense, then, to check the temperature each day before you choose what to wear. [141]

Heat and Energy

These girls are wearing heavy coats, mittens,
and hats to insulate their bodies.

How Heat Moves

The wind is blowing, and you feel cold. How do you warm up? You put on heavy socks, a coat, a hat,[25] and gloves. Your clothes become insulators against the cold. Insulators keep heat from moving. Your clothes are insulators that keep your body heat from moving[50] away from your body. Most homes have insulation, too. Home insulation keeps cold air outside in the winter and hot air outside in the summer.[75]

Because insulators keep heat from moving from place to place, they are bad conductors. Conductors let heat move easily from place to place. Metals are[100] good conductors. To test this, put a metal spoon into warm water. The spoon becomes warm as it conducts the heat in the water to[125] your hand. A wooden spoon works better to stir something warm because wood is not a good conductor.[143]

Heat and Energy

Write words that will help you remember what you learned.

Generating Heat

_____

_____

_____

_____

Temperature

_____

_____

_____

_____

Growing Larger and Smaller

_____

_____

_____

_____

Heat in Black and White

_____

_____

_____

_____

How Heat Moves

_____

_____

_____

_____

Generating Heat

1. "Generating Heat" is MAINLY about _____

   Ⓐ changing food into friction.

   Ⓑ particles that make heat.

   Ⓒ how people make and use energy.

   Ⓓ why friction is generated.

2. Why do you feel hot when you ride your bike?

   _____

   _____

   _____

Temperature

1. What does temperature tell?

   Ⓐ how long something is

   Ⓑ what the weather will be

   Ⓒ what something is made of

   Ⓓ how cold or hot something is

2. How does a thermometer work that has liquid in a tube?

   _____

   _____

   _____

Heat and Energy

Growing Larger and Smaller

1. Sidewalks are built with small pieces of concrete because _____

   Ⓐ big pieces of concrete can expand unevenly and crack.

   Ⓑ small pieces of concrete generate friction when they rub together.

   Ⓒ big pieces of concrete are too heavy to handle.

   Ⓓ people need more energy to work with big pieces of concrete.

2. Why do liquids expand and contract?

   _____

   _____

   _____

Heat in Black and White

1. The main idea of "Heat in Black and White" is that _____

   Ⓐ light bounces off black clothing.

   Ⓑ light in hot climates is hotter than light in other places.

   Ⓒ light is absorbed by white clothing in winter.

   Ⓓ light acts differently on black materials than on white materials.

2. Why do people in hot climates often wear white clothes?

   _____

   _____

   _____

How Heat Moves

1. Which of the following best describes how an insulator works?

   Ⓐ An insulator keeps heat from moving.

   Ⓑ Heat moves through an insulator.

   Ⓒ An insulator attracts heat.

   Ⓓ Heat is spread out by an insulator.

2. What is the difference between an insulator and a conductor?

   _____

   _____

   _____

🧩 Connect Your Ideas

1. Tell about two ways to get warm that were described in these passages.

   _____

   _____

   _____

2. The liquid in a thermometer is going down. Tell what makes that happen and why it happens.

   _____

   _____

   _____

The Laws of Motion

DÉCOUVERTE DE LA THÉORIE DE LA GRAVITATION UNIVERSELLE.

CACAO PUR HOLLANDAIS BENSDORP AMSTERDAM (Hollande)

This painting shows Isaac Newton sitting in the garden at his home in England.

Force and Motion

Motion happens when something moves from one place to another. Every motion is the result of a force that pushes or pulls[25] something. Force is also needed to stop something that is in motion.

A bicycle shows how force and motion work. A person pushes the bike's[50] pedals to make it start moving. Once the bike is moving, it takes force to stop it. The brakes create the force that stops the[75] bike.

More than 300 years ago, a scientist named Isaac Newton identified three laws that explain how force and motion work. Newton understood that some[100] forces, such as gravity, can cause motion from a distance. For example, even though Earth is far from the Moon, Earth's gravity exerts a force[125] on the Moon. Many modern inventions, including airplanes, rockets, and seatbelts, show Newton's laws of motion at work.[143]

The Laws of Motion

Some kind of force would be needed
to overcome inertia and move this rock.

The First Law: Inertia

A rock can sit on a mountainside for hundreds, even thousands, of years. However, if a landslide or an earthquake gets [25] it moving, the rock will roll until something stops it.

Newton's first law of motion describes the rock at rest and in motion. This law [50] is called the law of inertia. Whether an object is at rest or in motion, inertia means that the object stays in that state unless [75] an outside force acts on it.

The law of inertia explains why everyone should wear seatbelts in cars. When the driver of a car slams [100] on the brakes, the people inside the car keep traveling at the speed at which the car was moving. The brakes stop the car, but [125] the bodies inside it stay in motion. Seatbelts stop the people from moving forward—through the car's windshield. [143]

The Laws of Motion

The force this baseball player is using will
control the acceleration of the ball.

The Second Law: Acceleration

The size and weight of a baseball do not change. However, a baseball player might hit a ball three feet one[25] time and hundreds of feet the next time. The difference is the force he or she uses. The force of the bat on the ball[50] controls how far and how fast the ball travels.

Newton's second law explains the effect of force on the baseball's acceleration. *Acceleration* means "a change[75] in speed." A strong force changes the acceleration of an object, such as a baseball, more than a weak force does.

The mass of an[100] object changes acceleration, too. Suppose a baseball player hits a bowling ball and a baseball with the same force. Because the bowling ball has a[125] greater mass, it won't go as far as the baseball, even if the batter uses the same force.[143]

The Laws of Motion

The space shuttle blasts off because of the
actions and reactions created by its fuel.

The Third Law:
Action and Reaction

Before a rocket blasts off, scientists light the fuel at its base. The burning fuel gives off hot gases[25] that expand quickly. These gases create an action force. The rocket reacts to this force by pushing forward. In this way, the reaction force pushes[50] the rocket upward.

The action and reaction forces that move a rocket show Newton's third law of motion. This law states that every push or[75] pull results in a push or pull in the opposite direction. This opposite, or reaction, force is equal in strength to the action force.

While[100] space scientists use action and reaction forces to get rockets moving, other scientists use these forces to keep things in balance. For example, the weight[125] of the parts of a bridge that push down balances the weight of the parts that push up.[143]

The Laws of Motion

Putting a lubricant on a bike chain can reduce
friction and help the rider move faster.

Friction

A person wearing socks can slide on a hardwood floor but not on a carpet. The reason is friction. There is less friction between[25] socks and a hardwood floor than between socks and a carpet. If there is little friction between two surfaces, the surfaces easily slide past each[50] other.

Friction occurs whenever two surfaces rub against each other. This is because most surfaces have tiny bumps. When the bumps on one surface touch[75] the bumps on another surface, movement slows. In this way, friction slows or stops movement.

A slippery substance called a lubricant helps surfaces slide past[100] each other. One kind of lubricant is oil. Oil reduces friction between the metal surfaces of a bicycle, helping the bicycle to move smoothly.

Yet[125] friction is helpful, too. The brakes of a bicycle create friction between the brake and wheel, stopping the bicycle.[144]

The Laws of Motion

Write words that will help you remember what you learned.

Force and Motion

_____

_____

_____

_____

The First Law: Inertia

_____

_____

_____

_____

The Second Law: Acceleration

_____

_____

_____

The Third Law: Action and Reaction

_____

_____

_____

Friction

_____

_____

_____

_____

Force and Motion

1. "Force and Motion" is MAINLY about _____

   (A) why things start and stop moving.

   (B) how to use gravity and force.

   (C) modern inventions based on Isaac Newton's ideas.

   (D) how to stop things that are in motion.

2. What are force and motion?

   _____

   _____

   _____

The First Law: Inertia

1. The law of inertia explains _____

   (A) why people should study rocks.

   (B) how seatbelts keep people safe in cars.

   (C) why force and motion cause earthquakes.

   (D) how Isaac Newton created the laws of motion.

2. Explain the law of inertia.

   _____

   _____

   _____

The Laws of Motion

The Second Law: Acceleration

1. What does the word *acceleration* mean?

   Ⓐ a change in size

   Ⓑ a change in speed

   Ⓒ a change in force

   Ⓓ a change in motion

2. Explain the law of acceleration.

   _____

   _____

   _____

The Third Law: Action and Reaction

1. Which of the following shows action and reaction?

   Ⓐ a bike moving on a roadway

   Ⓑ a rocket blasting into space

   Ⓒ two baseballs traveling at the same speed

   Ⓓ hot gases that stay in one place

2. Explain the law of action and reaction.

   _____

   _____

   _____

Friction

1. When does friction occur?

   (A) when one thing is heavier than another

   (B) when one thing falls faster than another

   (C) when two things rub together

   (D) when a thing remains in motion

2. When is friction useful? When is it not useful?

   _____

   _____

   _____

Connect Your Ideas

1. How do two of Newton's laws of motion help you ride a bike?

   _____

   _____

   _____

2. Give two other examples of how you see Newton's laws of motion working in everyday life.

   _____

   _____

   _____

The Middle Ages

This castle was built in England during the 1300s.

The Feudal System

Many stories tell about castles and knights who lived in what is now Europe. The Middle Ages was a time of real[25] castles and knights. However, most people during the Middle Ages were serfs who worked in fields, not knights who lived in castles.

The system of[50] government during the Middle Ages was called *feudal*, which means "land." A few kings were at the top of the feudal system. These kings gave[75] land to lords, whose armies fought in the kings' wars. The lords gave land to knights, who fought in the lords' armies. The lords and[100] knights let serfs farm their land. In return, the serfs gave most of their crops to the lords and knights.

The Middle Ages began when[125] the Roman Empire ended in 475. The Middle Ages ended around 1500, when national governments replaced the feudal system.[144]

The Middle Ages

This picture, which was painted in the 1500s,
shows serfs farming on a lord's manor.

Life on a Manor

Because there were few cities in Europe during the Middle Ages, most people lived on the manors of lords. A manor[25] contained the lord's house or castle, fields for crops and cattle, and a village of houses for serfs. Both serfs and their cattle lived in[50] the small houses. Tools, shoes, and cloth were sold in the village shops.

The lord had power over everyone on the manor. Although serfs farmed[75] the land, the lord owned everything, including the serfs' houses and cattle. Lords promised to protect their serfs, but serfs had to fight when the[100] lord's land was attacked.

In addition to owning everything, lords made the laws on their manors. They acted as judges when laws were broken and[125] carried out punishments. If a lord's laws or punishments were unfair, serfs could do nothing to get better treatment.[144]

The Middle Ages

This picture, which was painted in the 1400s, shows a lord's army marching into battle. The wagon holds supplies for the army.

Warfare

During the Middle Ages, many wars were fought over land. Lords were always ready to defend their land from attacks by other lords. Lords[25] prepared for these attacks by building large castles, often on hills. Soldiers who watched from the high castle walls could see their enemies coming and[50] prepare.

Most of the soldiers in the lords' armies were their serfs. The serfs had no horses or armor, little training in warfare, and poor[75] weapons.

In contrast, the knights who led the armies had at least 14 years of training in warfare. They had the best weapons, horses, and[100] armor to protect their bodies.

The lord's first defenses were his castle's design and his serfs' skill in fighting. However, if enemy soldiers got inside[125] the castle, the lord's success depended on his skill and the skill of his knights.[140]

The Middle Ages

These serfs are enjoying a festival on one of their few holidays.

Festivals

Serfs in the Middle Ages worked from sunrise to sunset every day except Sundays and holy days. Holy days, or holidays, began as church[25] events. However, holidays became times for feasting, or festivals, when the serfs did not work.

People enjoyed themselves in many ways at festivals. They bought[50] food, drinks, and items such as cloth and pots and pans. Musicians sang songs that told stories. People danced as musicians played pipes, drums, and[75] lutes. Some musicians had bears that danced to music.

Like comedians today, jesters in the Middle Ages told jokes and funny stories. Unlike most comedians[100] today, however, jesters dressed like clowns and did tricks, such as juggling balls. Crowds especially liked acrobats, who balanced on the edge of swords or[125] on high ropes. While acrobats balanced on ropes, they also did tricks, such as swallowing fire.[141]

The printing press allowed ideas to spread more quickly because people no longer had to copy books by hand.

The End of the Middle Ages

The Renaissance or "new birth" followed the Middle Ages. The Renaissance brought new ideas in science and art. These[25] ideas were spread by printing presses, which printed books much faster than people could copy them by hand. In this way, printing presses helped the[50] Renaissance to grow.

A disease called the Black Death, or the plague, also helped to end the Middle Ages. One-third of the people in[75] Europe died from the plague in just a few years. Fleas spread the plague by biting infected rats. People got the plague by being bitten[100] by infected fleas.

In many villages, almost all of the people died. With fewer people to work the lords' lands, serfs could ask for better[125] treatment, such as the right to own their own land. As the serfs were freed, the feudal system ended.[144]

The Middle Ages

Write words that will help you remember what you learned.

The Feudal System

_____

_____

_____

_____

Life on a Manor

_____

_____

_____

_____

Warfare

_____

_____

_____

_____

Festivals

_____

_____

_____

_____

The End of the Middle Ages

_____

_____

_____

_____

The Feudal System

1. Another good name for "The Feudal System" is _____

   Ⓐ "Wars in the Middle Ages."

   Ⓑ "Farmers and Knights."

   Ⓒ "Kings, Lords, Knights, and Serfs."

   Ⓓ "Castles in the Middle Ages."

2. Describe the feudal system.

_____

_____

_____

Life on a Manor

1. Which of the following describes the lord of the manor?

   Ⓐ He had power over everything on the manor.

   Ⓑ He sold things in the shops on the manor.

   Ⓒ He lived in the village and protected his lands.

   Ⓓ He farmed his fields by himself.

2. Describe how a lord ruled his manor.

_____

_____

_____

The Middle Ages

Warfare

1. "Warfare" is MAINLY about _____

   Ⓐ the wars between serfs and knights during the Middle Ages.

   Ⓑ how wars today are like wars during the Middle Ages.

   Ⓒ how wars were fought during the Middle Ages.

   Ⓓ the weapons invented during the Middle Ages.

2. Why were many wars fought during the Middle Ages?

   _____

   _____

   _____

Festivals

1. "Festivals" is MAINLY about _____

   Ⓐ why lords allowed serfs to go to festivals.

   Ⓑ how serfs enjoyed themselves at festivals.

   Ⓒ how much time serfs worked during the year.

   Ⓓ why only men were allowed to go to festivals.

2. What were three ways serfs enjoyed themselves at festivals during the Middle Ages?

   _____

   _____

   _____

The End of the Middle Ages

1. The Renaissance was a time when _____

    Ⓐ the feudal system learned how to make printing presses.

    Ⓑ the kings, lords, and knights had more power over the serfs.

    Ⓒ people had new ideas and information spread more quickly.

    Ⓓ the Roman Empire came to an end in Europe.

2. Describe how an invention and a disease helped to end the Middle Ages.

_____

_____

_____

Connect Your Ideas

1. Describe the life of a serf in the Middle Ages.

_____

_____

_____

2. Compare how people in the United States live today with how people in Europe lived during the Middle Ages.

_____

_____

_____

The American Civil War

The top picture shows cotton being packed in the South. The bottom picture shows a factory in the North using cotton to make cloth.

The Civil War Begins

Although the United States was less than 100 years old, it was a troubled country. The South's income came mostly from[25] farming, especially cotton farming. Cotton was cheap to grow if enslaved people worked the fields. The North's income came from businesses that did not use[50] slavery, including banks and railroads. Because the states could not agree on slavery and other things, they went to war.

When the United States was[75] formed, five of the 13 states demanded that slavery remain legal. As new states were added, the North and South argued about whether slavery should[100] be legal in these places.

In 1860, the South believed that the new president, Abraham Lincoln, would make slavery illegal, so 11 states formed their[125] own country. They called their country the Confederate States of America. The 22 remaining states were called the Union.[144]

The American Civil War

In this picture, the Union and Confederate armies
are fighting at Gettysburg, Pennsylvania.

The Battle of Gettysburg

In the spring of 1861, the Confederate army fired on Fort Sumter, a Union fort, and the Civil War began. After[25] that, the two armies fought many battles.

Until July 1863, fighting occurred mostly in Confederate states or in Union states that had allowed slavery, such[50] as Kentucky. In July 1863, however, the Confederate army invaded the North. It met the Union army at Gettysburg, Pennsylvania. During three days of fighting,[75] about 51,000 soldiers died.

The Battle of Gettysburg was a turning point in the war. After that Pennsylvania battle, the Confederate army retreated south and[100] did not invade the North again.

In November 1863, President Lincoln gave a speech at Gettysburg to honor the dead soldiers. He ended his speech[125] by saying that "government of the people, by the people, for the people, shall not perish from the Earth."[144]

The American Civil War

African American soldiers fought bravely in the Union army. This soldier won the Medal of Honor.

Civil War Soldiers

The Civil War divided families, too. Especially in Union states such as Kentucky, which had allowed slavery, people in the same family[25] held opposing views. Sometimes, brothers fought opposite one another.

Soldiers in both armies started the war with enough supplies. Union soldiers wore blue uniforms, while[50] Confederate soldiers wore gray uniforms. Soldiers had food, backpacks, and new rifles. However, as the war continued, supplies became scarce. Many soldiers had torn uniforms[75] and no shoes.

Many freed slaves joined the Union army. But even as freed men, African American and white soldiers were put into separate units.[100] In addition, African Americans were given old uniforms and rifles and poor supplies. However, African American units fought bravely.

American losses were greater during the[125] Civil War than in any other war. More than one million soldiers died or were wounded.[141]

The American Civil War

Johnny Clem was a young drummer boy in the
Union army during the American Civil War.

Children in the Civil War

After their fathers and brothers left to fight in the Civil War, many children had to work on farms and[25] in businesses. Even children as young as 11 and 12 years old served in the army, often as drummers. Drummers beat out the officers' commands[50] because soldiers could not hear their officers in the noise of battle. The drumbeats told the soldiers which way to go.

When the war began,[75] men had to be at least 18 years old to join either army. However, with no system for checking birth dates, younger boys who said[100] that they were 18 often became soldiers.

At its largest, the Confederate army was half the size of the Union army. As the war went[125] on and more soldiers were needed, however, the Confederate army accepted boys as young as 14 years old.[143]

The American Civil War

General Robert E. Lee, the leader of the Confederate army,
is shown surrendering to General Ulysses S. Grant, the leader
of the Union army. General Lee, with white hair and beard,
is seated at the left. General Grant is signing a paper.

After the War

In April 1865, General Robert E. Lee, the leader of the Confederate army, surrendered to General Ulysses S. Grant, the leader of[25] the Union army. Ulysses S. Grant told the Union soldiers not to celebrate, but to treat the Confederate soldiers as their fellow countrymen.

However, the[50] country did not have time to celebrate the end of the war. Less than a week after General Lee surrendered, President Abraham Lincoln was killed[75] by John Wilkes Booth, who was angry at the outcome of the war. President Lincoln would not be able to bring the country back together.[100]

After the war, the South faced many hardships. New sources of income were needed. The land had not been farmed, so food was scarce. Also,[125] although slavery was illegal, opposing views about race remained. It would take the United States many years to heal.[144]

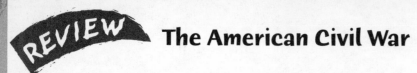

REVIEW The American Civil War

Write words that will help you remember what you learned.

The Civil War Begins

_____

_____

_____

_____

The Battle of Gettysburg

_____

_____

_____

_____

Civil War Soldiers

_____

_____

_____

_____

Children in the Civil War

_____

_____

_____

_____

After the War

_____

_____

_____

_____

The Civil War Begins

1. How did the North and South get their income before the Civil War?

   Ⓐ The North's income came from slavery, but the South's did not.

   Ⓑ Both the North and South got their income from banks and cotton.

   Ⓒ The South's income came from slavery, but the North's did not.

   Ⓓ Both the North and the South got their incomes from the Union.

2. Compare what people in the North and the South thought about slavery.

   _____

   _____

   _____

The Battle of Gettysburg

1. At Gettysburg, President Lincoln gave a speech that honored all of the soldiers who fought _____

   Ⓐ in the Civil War.

   Ⓑ for the Union army.

   Ⓒ and died in Pennsylvania.

   Ⓓ for the Confederate army.

2. Why was the Battle of Gettysburg important?

   _____

   _____

   _____

The American Civil War

Civil War Soldiers

1. Which of the following is true of soldiers during the Civil War?

   Ⓐ Soldiers on both sides always had enough supplies.

   Ⓑ Some brothers fought on opposite sides in the war.

   Ⓒ Many freed slaves joined the Confederate army.

   Ⓓ All soldiers had blue uniforms, rifles, and backpacks.

2. How were African American soldiers and white soldiers in the Union army treated differently?

   _____

   _____

   _____

Children in the Civil War

1. The main idea of "Children in the Civil War" is that _____

   Ⓐ children worked on farms during the Civil War.

   Ⓑ children were soldiers in the Confederate army.

   Ⓒ children served in both armies during the Civil War.

   Ⓓ children could not serve in either army during the Civil War.

2. Describe two ways in which children served during the Civil War.

   _____

   _____

   _____

After the War

1. "After the War" is MAINLY about _____

   (A) how the United States healed after the Civil War.

   (B) why General Lee surrendered to General Grant.

   (C) why President Abraham Lincoln was killed.

   (D) what happened when the Civil War was over.

2. Why do you think General Grant told the Union soldiers not to celebrate winning the Civil War?

   _____

   _____

   _____

Connect Your Ideas

1. Tell three facts about the soldiers who fought in the Civil War.

   _____

   _____

   _____

2. Suppose it was your job to bring the North and South together after the Civil War. Tell about two things you would do.

   _____

   _____

   _____

Ancient Civilizations of the Americas

Archaeologists study people of long ago
by looking for things people left behind.

Three Ancient Civilizations

Columbus and other explorers are often described as discovering America. However, many civilizations existed in the Americas for hundreds of years before[25] Columbus and other explorers arrived. These ancient civilizations include the Anasazi of North America, the Mayas of Central America, and the Incas of South America.[50]

The people in all three civilizations were great builders, even without the machines that exist today. Each civilization had other strengths, too. The Anasazi farmed[75] and made beautiful baskets. The Mayas used mathematics and had a system of writing. The Incas built many miles of roads.

Archaeologists are scientists who[100] study how people in ancient times lived. Archaeologists gather information about the Anasazi, Mayas, and Incas by digging where these groups lived. Each time archaeologists[125] find pictures or writing on a rock, they learn about the people who lived in the Americas long ago.[144]

Ancient Civilizations of the Americas

The Anasazi built homes into cliffs to keep themselves safe from attack.

The Anasazi

From about 100 B.C. to A.D. 1300, the Anasazi lived in what is now the southwest United States. The Anasazi were great builders,[25] building miles of roads for trading with people far away.

The Anasazi also built large buildings in cliffs. The cliffs kept the Anasazi safe from[50] attack. Similar to modern apartments, Anasazi buildings housed as many as 1,000 people. One apartment building, called Pueblo Bonito, had more than 800 rooms. For[75] almost 1,000 years, Pueblo Bonito was the largest building in North America.

In about A.D. 1300, the Anasazi left their cities. No one knows why.[100] There was a drought, so perhaps they left to find water. Their cities may have become too crowded. It's also possible that the Anasazi farmed[125] so much that their land became useless. Archaeologists are looking for clues about why the Anasazi civilization disappeared.[143]

Ancient Civilizations of the Americas

This Mayan pyramid, which was built hundreds of years ago, is still standing today.

The Mayas

The Mayan civilization, which lasted from about 1500 B.C. to about A.D. 1500, reached from present-day Mexico into Central America. Although Egypt[25] was far away, the Mayan and Egyptian civilizations were similar in some ways.

Like the Egyptians, the Mayas built pyramids. These pyramids were built by[50] fitting stones together tightly. Some Mayan pyramids are still standing today. In fact, until 1902, the tallest building in North America was a Mayan pyramid.[75]

The Mayas used a writing system with pictures and signs called hieroglyphics. Ancient Egyptians also wrote with hieroglyphics. Archaeologists have learned about both civilizations by[100] reading their hieroglyphics.

The Mayas had a vast knowledge of science and mathematics. By studying the stars and Sun, Mayan scientists observed that a year[125] has 365 days. The Mayas were also among the first to use the idea of zero in mathematics.[143]

Ancient Civilizations of the Americas

This Incan town was built high in the mountains of present-day South America.

The Incas

The Incan civilization developed on the northwest coast of present-day South America. Unlike the Mayan civilization, the Incan civilization was short-lived,[25] only lasting from about A.D. 1200 to 1533.

The Incan government was rich and strong. The people paid taxes to the government, even though the[50] Incas didn't use money. Instead, the Incan government took people's work and the crops they grew as payment.

The Incas also had to do a[75] certain amount of work for the government each year. One kind of government work was building roads. The Incas built more than 14,000 miles of[100] roads. This system of roads made traveling and trade easier.

The Incas did not have a written language. Instead, they sent messages by using a[125] messenger system. Messengers traveled many miles on Incan roads, helping to connect the cities in the Incan civilization.[143]

Ancient Civilizations of the Americas

These pictures show that the kinds of baskets the Anasazi made long ago are still being made today. The woman is from the Hopi group.

Where Are They Now?

The Anasazi, Mayan, and Incan civilizations no longer exist. However, in parts of the Americas, some groups today live in similar [25] ways to those of these ancient civilizations.

The Zuni and Hopi groups in the southwest United States weave baskets and make pots like those made [50] by the Anasazi. Because of these shared practices, some archaeologists think that the Anasazi did not disappear but, instead, moved to new places and formed [75] new groups, such as the Zuni and Hopi.

The Mayan civilization that built pyramids and made scientific discoveries has disappeared. However, some people in Mexico [100] and Central America call themselves Mayas, speak Mayan, and practice the Mayan religion. Similarly, some people in South America speak the Incan language and practice [125] the Incan religion. Because of these likenesses, archaeologists think that present-day groups have descended from the ancient civilizations. [144]

REVIEW Ancient Civilizations of the Americas

Write words that will help you remember what you learned.

Three Ancient Civilizations

_____

_____

_____

_____

The Anasazi

_____

_____

_____

_____

The Mayas

_____

_____

_____

The Incas

_____

_____

_____

Where Are They Now?

_____

_____

_____

_____

Three Ancient Civilizations

1. Which of the following is true of the ancient Anasazi, Mayan, and Incan civilizations?

Ⓐ The people were great mathematicians.

Ⓑ All three civilizations still exist today.

Ⓒ The people were great builders.

Ⓓ All three civilizations existed in Europe long ago.

2. How do people today learn about ancient civilizations?

_____

_____

_____

The Anasazi

1. Which of the following is a fact about the Anasazi?

Ⓐ They built houses in cliffs.

Ⓑ They were great musicians.

Ⓒ They were skilled archaeologists.

Ⓓ They did not farm their land.

2. Name one reason archaeologists think the Anasazi civilization disappeared.

_____

_____

_____

 **Ancient Civilizations of the Americas**

The Mayas

1. What did the Mayas learn by studying the stars and Sun?

   Ⓐ that they could write with hieroglyphics

   Ⓑ that they could build miles of roads

   Ⓒ that pyramids could be built on cliffs

   Ⓓ that one year has 365 days

2. What are two ways the Mayas were like the ancient Egyptians?

   _____

   _____

   _____

The Incas

1. How did the Incas send information to each other?

   Ⓐ by writing letters

   Ⓑ by messenger

   Ⓒ by sending newspapers

   Ⓓ by using hieroglyphics

2. Describe how the Incas paid taxes.

   _____

   _____

   _____

Where Are They Now?

1. "Where Are They Now?" is MAINLY about _____

   Ⓐ how strong the three civilizations are today.

   Ⓑ why the three civilizations disappeared.

   Ⓒ how the three civilizations are linked to people today.

   Ⓓ why most people in South America formed new groups.

2. Where do archaeologists think the Anasazi, Mayan, and Incan people are today?

   _____

   _____

   _____

Connect Your Ideas

1. Describe one thing that was built by each of the three ancient civilizations.

   _____

   _____

   _____

2. Name one way in which life in one of the three ancient civilizations you've read about is like life today. Name one way in which it is different.

   _____

   _____

   _____

Reading Log • Level E • Book 3

	I Read This	New Words I Learned	New Facts I Learned	What Else I Want to Learn About This Subject
How Light Works				
The Colors of Light				
The Speed of Light				
Light and Shadows				
Laser Beams				
Light Tricks				
Heat and Energy				
Generating Heat				
Temperature				
Growing Larger and Smaller				
Heat in Black and White				
How Heat Moves				
The Laws of Motion				
Force and Motion				
The First Law: Inertia				
The Second Law: Acceleration				
The Third Law: Action and Reaction				
Friction				

	I Read This	New Words I Learned	New Facts I Learned	What Else I Want to Learn About This Subject
The Middle Ages				
The Feudal System				
Life on a Manor				
Warfare				
Festivals				
The End of the Middle Ages				
The American Civil War				
The Civil War Begins				
The Battle of Gettysburg				
Civil War Soldiers				
Children in the Civil War				
After the War				
Ancient Civilizations of the Americas				
Three Ancient Civilizations				
The Anasazi				
The Mayas				
The Incas				
Where Are They Now?				

Self-Check Graph

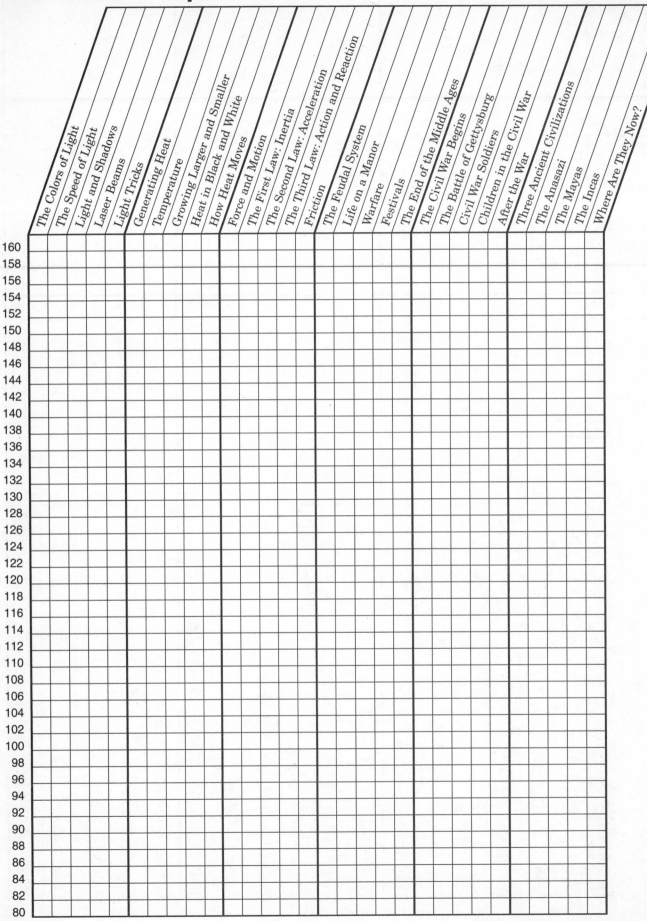

	The Colors of Light	The Speed of Light	Light and Shadows	Laser Beams	Light Tricks	Generating Heat	Temperature	Growing Larger and Smaller	Heat in Black and White	How Heat Moves	Force and Motion	The First Law: Inertia	The Second Law: Acceleration	The Third Law: Action and Reaction	Friction	The Feudal System	Life on a Manor	Warfare	Festivals	The End of the Middle Ages	The Civil War Begins	The Battle of Gettysburg	Civil War Soldiers	Children in the Civil War	After the War	Three Ancient Civilizations	The Anasazi	The Mayas	The Incas	Where Are They Now?
160																														
158																														
156																														
154																														
152																														
150																														
148																														
146																														
144																														
142																														
140																														
138																														
136																														
134																														
132																														
130																														
128																														
126																														
124																														
122																														
120																														
118																														
116																														
114																														
112																														
110																														
108																														
106																														
104																														
102																														
100																														
98																														
96																														
94																														
92																														
90																														
88																														
86																														
84																														
82																														
80																														